17,95

W9-ASX-514

WRITTEN BY
BRIGITTE COPPIN, MARIELLE DE BRISOULT,
ALAIN DUPAS, DOMINIQUE JOLY,
CATHERINE DE SAIRIGNÉ, JEAN-PIERRE VERDET

COVER DESIGN BY
STEPHANIE BLUMENTHAL

TRANSLATED AND ADAPTED BY
PAULA SCHANILEC AND ROSEMARY WALLNER

PUBLISHED BY CREATIVE EDUCATION
123 South Broad Street, Mankato, Minnesota 56001
Creative Education is an imprint of The Creative Company

Library of Congress Cataloging-in-Publication Data
[De decouvertes en inventions. English]
Inventing our world / by Brigitte Coppin et al. ; [illustrated by Paul Botemps et al. ;
translated and adapted by Paula Schanilec and Rosemary Wallner].
(Creative Discoveries) Includes index.
Summary: Traces the history of inventions from prehistoric times to the present.
ISBN: 0-88682-948-8
1. Inventions—History—Juvenile literature.   [1. Inventions—History.]
I. Coppin, Brigitte.   II. Botemps, Paul, ill.   III. Title.   IV. Series.
T15. D3413   1999
609—dc21   97-27525

First edition

2 4 6 8 9 7 5 3 1

INVENTING OUR WORLD

CONTENTS

CREATIVE EDUCATION

Many inventions and discoveries have been made since the days of the first humans. This book would not exist if reading and writing had not been invented. Before you picked it up, many people worked on this book. Some of the techniques they used to create it were invented several centuries ago; some are modern.

Thousands of years have passed since people first learned to mill flour and make use of the strength of animals.

First, the paper was made. Then the text was written, by hand or with the help of a computer. The pictures were drawn and colored. Photographic color plates were made from them. Once the books had been printed and bound, they were loaded into trucks and delivered to the publisher who sold them to bookstores and libraries. If you bought this copy, you probably used dollar bills and coins. Money is another invention.

People began to build primitive houses for shelter.

Just imagine what life must have been like 10,000 years ago. There was no money, no writing, no electricity, no wheels, nor engines to take you from one place to another. All these inventions, which we now take for granted, have transformed the way we look at the world. Sitting in homes, many people do not worry about heat or cold. Aches and pains and long distances are no longer the problems they once were because now we have things like central heating, medicines, telephones, and airplanes.

The first discoveries and inventions

Ten thousand years ago, humans had already invented the bow and arrow and the spear to hunt animals for food and clothing. They were beginning to domesticate the ox and the horse, and they had probably built simple rafts to cross rivers. But, most important of all, they had discovered fire. (They had discovered fire, not invented it, because fire exists in nature—perhaps early humans saw lightning strike and start a forest fire.)

Even today, South American Indians are skillful hunters and fishers using only a bow and arrow.

Many civilizations thought that fire was sacred, a gift from the gods. First people learned to keep a fire going, then how to start one by rubbing stones or pieces of dry wood together to make a spark. They began using fire to cook bread, to forge tools and weapons, and to bake pottery for storing grain or oil. Soon people swapped their stored, extra corn for goods they could not make themselves: trade had been born.

Barter was the first form of trade.

What does "barter" mean? If you swap some marbles for some stickers, or a comic book for some candy, then you're bartering with your friends! "Bartering" means exchanging things of similar value.

Barter was the first form of trade. In the illustration below on the right, an Egyptian farmer exchanges a goose, which he raised on the farm, for a clay pot at a market. In ancient Egypt, a monetary system did not exist.

Bartering has gone on since very early times.

What are coins, currency, checks, and credit cards used for? To buy things, of course. They are all forms of money. You can exchange money for things you cannot produce yourself: books and toys, food and clothes, or travel by bus or train.

Today, money is used for all kinds of business and trade. You may still hear people talking about silver and gold. Coins were once the only forms of money. But coins are no longer made from pure precious metals. Now you can pay not only with coins but with checks, money orders, and plastic cards too. Let's take a look at how money came to be invented.

Two roosters are passed . . .

. . . from hand to hand as each person . . .

. . . exchanges them for something.

In some countries, people used oxen or shells for money.

Some of the objects people used as money were rather bulky, like these slabs of copper the Phoenicians used.

For a long time, the African people used cowrie shells as money. The shells were light and easy to count.

The trouble with bartering is that no item has a definite value. What could the Egyptian farmer have done if the potter had not wanted his goose, or if he had demanded something else as well? And with the barter system it was impossible to save! There had to be another way.

How money began

Throughout history, different societies have chosen different objects to use as money. People have used dried fish, bars of salt, cooking pots, cattle—whatever was chosen had a fixed value. A sword might be worth two head of oxen and a jar of wine worth only one. But soon it became clear that using pieces of precious metal, which could be cut up and weighed, was really much more practical.

Most often, coins were made from gold, silver, and copper. All three of these metals can be found in the ground in a pure state, not hidden within another mineral. They are known as native metals. They do not wear down easily and are hard to find; even a tiny piece of gold is worth a great deal.

It was not long before gold became the symbol of wealth. It glitters as it catches the light, and it is easy to mold into different shapes and patterns. The quest for gold led people such as Christopher Columbus to unknown, distant lands. In Peru, in South America, the Spanish conquistadores looted the gold and silver of the Inca Indians and exploited their mineral mines.

In Ancient Rome, the value of objects was measured in cattle.

Aztec Indians in South America used cocoa beans as money. One rabbit might be worth 10 beans.

Gold and silver nuggets were made into coins.

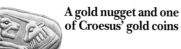

A gold nugget and one of Croesus' gold coins

Cretan coin   Carthaginian coin   Athenian coin

As rich as Croesus!

Croesus was the king of Lydia, now part of Turkey, and was famous for his riches. Croesus invented coins. His people hammered nuggets of gold and silver into shape, then stamped the new coins with a mark to show what they were worth. There was no longer any need to weigh the coins. Trade with other countries became simple.

The ancient Persians, Greeks, and Romans also minted their own coins. The designs they used tell us about their history. Coins from ancient Crete showed the famous maze at Knossos. The people of Athens stamped their coins with an owl, which was sacred to their goddess Athena.

The river Pactolus flows through Lydia. People collected nuggets of electrum, a mixture of gold and silver.

In Ancient Greece, the silver mines were worked by slaves.

How did people make coins? Below is a European workshop during the Middle Ages. The coins were first cut from sheets of metal, then struck between two engraved tools that pressed the design onto them. In those days, many people made coins, but the quality of the coins varied. Money changers had the job of checking the coins. They tapped them to see if they rang true, and weighed them on scales. Good coins were sound and full weight.

There were certain drawbacks to having coins made of real gold and silver. Counterfeiters copied the coins and made imitation ones out of worthless metal. In some countries, crooks caught making fake coins were put to death!

Clippers scraped and filed the coins to obtain slivers of the precious metal, which they would sell.

People used heavy, screw-down coin presses like this one in the 12th century. Today, machines powered by electricity press coins.

Since the 17th century, coins have had a clear-cut edge, sometimes grooved, so that people could not file them down. This modern Italian coin is made from two different metals.

Coins today have a lower value than they had in the past.
We use checks and credit cards to pay large sums of money, but coins are useful for smaller purchases. Today they are made from alloys of copper, nickel, brass, and palladium. Look at a coin: you will see its value, lettering showing the currency of the country, and the date when it was put into circulation. On U.S. coins, one side shows a president's head, the other side a symbol of the United States. Check your piggy bank! Some of the coins may be quite old!

As goods were traded around the world, money spread too.

In the old world, money changers did many of the jobs of a modern bank.

They kept their customers' money in a safe place or invested it so that it increased.

1. A customer pays for goods with money.
2. The shopkeeper deposits the money and receives a bill of exchange.
3. The bill could be used to pay another merchant.
4. The bill could be exchanged for coins again.

The word "bank" come from *banco*, the Italian word for the money changer's bench.

Robbers were always after the gold and silver coins. They waylaid travelers and stole their money. It soon became much safer for merchants to leave their money in the care of a banker. In return, the banker handed over a signed piece of paper: a bill of exchange. The merchant used this bill to pay for other goods. Whoever had the bill of exchange could come to the banker and exchange it for the original sum of money. Modern banking had been born.

Dollar bills, checks, credit cards: all evolved from the original idea of a bill of exchange. In addition to bankers, there were moneylenders who charged interest rates that were often impossibly high for lenders to pay back. They were called usurers, and they were very unpopular.

The Pont-au-Change in Paris

In 1141, King Louis VII of France ordered that all the goldsmiths, silversmiths, and money changers should set up their counters along a bridge over the River Seine. It is called the Pont-au-Change (Exchange Bridge).

Currency: pieces of paper with purchasing power

In each country, the artist creates the design, and the engraver works it onto a metal plate. The note is printed front and back.

The background design of each bill is individually created by computer.   A watermark

At first, coins and bills represented a sum of gold or silver that had been handed to the bank for safekeeping. The amount of precious metal in the bank exactly equaled the bills and coins being used in business. Cash could be exchanged at the bank for pieces of gold. Sometimes bankers would cheat and print more currency than they had gold! When the fraud was discovered, they would go bankrupt. They were out of business.

Today only one bank, the central bank in each country, can issue paper currency and coins. This bank supervises the country's banking system. In balance to the cash in circulation, the central bank holds gold, money from other countries (known as foreign currency), and other valuable items.

Paper currency was soon widely used. There was no time limit to it, and all businesses accepted it.

The making of dollar bills is a delicate operation! The bill has to be difficult to copy and is made from special paper. Some currencies have watermarks to protect against counterfeiting. If you hold the bill up to the light, you will see the design and color of the watermark through it. The special printing process is kept a secret.

When dollar bills become dirty, torn, or damaged, the banks exchange them for new currency. The old bills are destroyed.

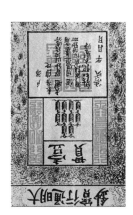

The Chinese began using paper money in the ninth century. The first currency carried the seal of the emperor.

Many people in France were ruined when the financier John Law went bankrupt in the 18th century. There were riots in the streets.

Money all over the world

The smallest paper currency in the world came from Morocco. It was the size of a postage stamp.

Every country has its own particular money: its currency. Travelers often exchange one national currency for another. To make this possible, banks around the world set up the exchange rate between the various currencies of different countries.

The rate varies every day depending on how strong the economy of the country is.

Today, most people put their money in a bank. Why? Because it is safe, and the bank can offer a range of other services.

When you deposit money in a bank, you are given a checkbook, which is a convenient way to pay. Banks can also lend you money.

Security firms transport large sums of money in armored vehicles.

You may have seen your parents or other adults writing a check. They fill in the date, the amount they want to pay, and the name of the person to whom they are paying the check. Then they sign it, to prove they wish to make the payment.

The person who receives the check sends it to the bank, and then the bank takes that amount of money from your parents' bank account and pays it to the person whose name is on the check.

The currency of the United States is the dollar.

The currency of Japan is the *yen*.

The currency of Belgium is the *Belgian franc*.

The currency of Germany is the *Deutschmark*.

The currency of Italy is the *lira*.

The currency of France is the *French franc*.

The currency of Spain is the *peseta*.

The currency of Holland is the *florin*.

The currency of Great Britain is the pound.

Often banks have a vault where their clients can store money, jewels, or other valuables.

A bank allows you to pay by credit.

If adults do not have enough money to buy a house or a car, the bank may lend them some: this is called credit. In exchange for this service, the adults will have to pay back the bank a sum larger than the sum they borrowed. The difference between the two sums is called interest.

Plastic credit cards work like a loan.

On the back of each card, you will see a magnetic band. This contains the card's memory, which allows it to identify the account to which the item's cost will be billed. Some credit card interest rates are high, so people should pay off credit cards bills right away to avoid those extra costs, which add up quickly. You can also use a plastic card to draw money from a cash machine, but for security reasons, these machines can only give out a certain amount of cash. Many people have credit cards so they don't have to carry a lot of cash with them.

The *Bourse*, the French Stock Exchange, was designed to look like a Greek temple. *Bourse* means "purse" in French.

The secret code in the card's memory is hidden in the magnetic band.

People use their credit card or cash card to draw money from cash machines, but first people have to type in the secret number that corresponds to their card.

Most people work to earn a living. In return for their work, they are paid money.

People deposit their money with a bank. The bank opens an account and provides a checkbook and cash card.

People with a bank account can pay for things with a check or a debit card, which works like a check but looks like a credit card.

The shopkeeper turns the check over to the bank and receives the amount on the check from the buyer's bank account.

People and countries trade because it supplies them with things that they are not able to produce themselves. For centuries, merchants have bought, sold, transported, and exchanged all kinds of goods all over the world. They went by sea and by river, and they crossed deserts and mountains.

Old world traders needed to move their goods as quickly and easily as possible. This is why roads and ports were built and larger and larger boats were developed. Markets began to spring up at the major crossroads and grow into towns. **The first great seafaring traders of the ancient Western world were the Phoenicians.** Their sturdy ships crisscrossed the Mediterranean Sea, bringing gold and ivory from Africa and lead and silver from Spain.

By the 13th century, the Italian merchants dominated trade with the East. Their heavy sailing ships reached Venice and Genoa at the end of their long voyages brimming with spices and bales of silk. Deals were done as soon as the merchants reached the quayside. Prices were high, because silk and spices from the Far East were in great demand in Europe, and only the wealthiest citizens and royalty could afford them.

Gradually, European sailors ventured farther and farther on uncharted seas. The Portuguese on board their caravels sailed around Africa to reach India and the Spice Islands. After Christopher Columbus landed in North America, the Spanish crossed the Atlantic and returned laden with gold and silver.

In Europe during the Middle Ages, merchants of the same trade gathered in covered halls built especially for them. There would be the cloth market, the corn exchange, the fish market, and so on.

Foreign goods appeared in Europe: coffee, tea, cocoa, sugarcane, and potatoes. Merchants grew rich and competed with each other to see who could finish a journey in the shortest time.

By the 17th century, the British and the Dutch had taken control of the trade route to India. They brought back diamonds and fine porcelain from China.

Towns and cities need a constant supply of goods.

At the time of the Industrial Revolution in the 1800s, towns were springing up quickly around the first big factories. Thousands of people moved from the country to cities, looking for work.

How were these people to be clothed and fed? Peddlers walked the streets with baskets of goods, but they couldn't supply all of the people's needs. Wholesale markets were needed.

Wholesale markets were open every day and even at night. Merchants and storekeepers came to buy in bulk. They took meat, fish, vegetables, and flowers back to their own stores to sell to people. Those days also saw the coming of larger stores—department stores. Customers could wander at ease from floor to floor. For the first time, prices were clearly marked on labels.

Entry was free, and you did not have to buy anything. Customers who did make a purchase could have their goods delivered by horse-drawn wagon, with posters on the side advertising the store.

By the 19th century, new forms of transport, such as trains and steamships, could move goods more quickly than ever before, but people still used the horse and cart.

Trade has brought jobs to millions of people. Think of how many people's hands a product passes through from the time it is made to the time it is bought by the final customer—you, for instance. Today, you find oranges, tomatoes, and strawberries in the stores even in midwinter. These fruits may have come from Mexico, Jamaica, or Chile! Every day, refrigerated trucks, ships, and cargo planes bring us fish, fresh fruit, and vegetables from distant countries around the world.

Advertising entices us to buy something! Glossy pictures in magazines, billboards along the streets, and mouth-watering images on TV screens are designed to persuade us to try a new toy or a dessert. If you go into a supermarket, the choice in every aisle is enormous. Each product claims that it is the best—bigger, better, more effective, new and improved. . . . How do you decide?

In some countries, a traveling salesperson will cook you a pancake made with eggs from his own hens.

The traditional way of selling things

Shopping used to be a way of meeting people, chatting, and exchanging news. Storekeepers and stall holders would be your friends. In many countries today, buying and selling still continue this same way. Farmers and artisans in Africa and South America still sell their goods at local markets. In Europe too, especially in the country, super-markets have not yet managed to replace the village stores or local farm shop.

An open-air market in South America

An African market under canvas

A shopping street in Far East Asia

A European store

Trade led to the invention of weights and measures.

To barter or sell, people needed to have an idea of the weight, length, and volume of the goods they wanted to exchange.

People first started to use measurements thousands of years ago. Ever since people could count, they have measured things by the span of a hand or a thumb's length. Feet or paces were useful for longer measurements.

In Egypt, fields were measured out using ropes 12 cubits long: a cubit was the distance from fingertips to elbow.

Desert peoples measured the distance between wells in terms of how far away they could hear a shout or shoot an arrow.

The foot is a common unit of measurement—although not many people have feet 12 inches long!

Ancient Egyptian ruler

From early times, people have tried to develop a system of measurements upon which everyone could agree. To make trade and tax collecting easier, kings in ancient times ordered traders and farmers in their kingdoms to use the same measurements. Known as standard measurements, these gave a fixed value to the length of a foot or a cubit and made trade simpler.

Both the Romans and the Egyptians used the palm of the hand —about three inches (7.5 cm)—as a unit of measurement.

Peasant farmers were not interested in the exact surface of a field; they preferred to measure it by the time it took to plow. In the Middle Ages, most products were measured in containers: they were sold by volume, not by weight. Merchants could cheat by not filling the containers properly. They might buy a jar of grain full to the brim, and resell it with an inch or two to spare at the top!

About 4,000 years ago, Egyptian peasants measured the harvest using a kind of barrel called a bushel. The measured grain was tipped into baskets and stored.

Builders buy wood in units called board feet.

Later, standard units were invented to check the containers used for measuring. The standards had to be kept in a safe place. Even so, many were falsified and people were cheated. Worse still, measurements often varied between different regions and different products. In Great Britain, for example, the bushel meant one thing in the city and another in the country, and a bushel of wheat was not equivalent to a bushel of oats.

There had to be a new way of measuring that was fair and common to all. At the end of the 18th century, scientists decided to find a measure that could not be altered, based on the Earth itself. The length of the Paris meridian was divided by 40 million, and in 1799, after seven years of calculations, the meter was born!

In medieval European markets, stone containers, which could not be moved, ensured a standard measure of grain.

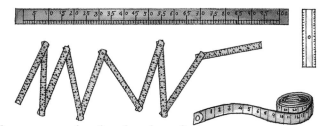

The meter is the basis of the international metric system. The meter can be divided or multiplied by 10. One meter equals 100 centimeters, and one kilometer equals 1,000 meters.

The United States is one of the few nations that does not use the metric system in daily life. But many U.S. businesses, especially those that trade with other countries, must use the metric system as well.

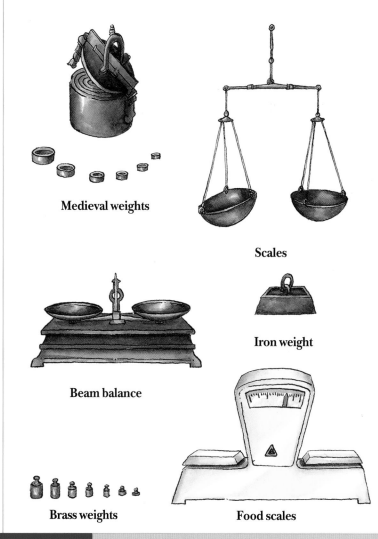

Medieval weights

Scales

Iron weight

Beam balance

Brass weights

Food scales

Measuring led to writing because quantities needed to be recorded. Writing was invented, in part, so that people could keep accounts of taxes and harvests. It also helped trade run smoothly.

The Western writing system was born in Sumer, in Mesopotamia—which is located in the Middle East—more than 5,000 years ago. To help people keep track of the offerings made at the temple, the priests who governed the city decided to use sharp sticks to mark off the number of flocks and harvest on tablets of soft clay. In other parts of the world, ancient people used knotted ropes, notched sticks, and other things to help them count, keep track of time, and measure distance.

The early writing of the Sumerians is called cuneiform, meaning wedge-shaped. It is made up of angles and wedge shapes arranged in different patterns. At first it took the form of drawings representing the object, which we call pictograms. These early drawings have been found on every continent except Antarctica.

To write the word "corn," one would draw an ear of grain. By putting two signs together, one could express a more complicated idea. For example, a bull's head placed next to a mountain would mean that the herds had come from the other side of the mountains. But there were too many symbols to learn. Writing had to be simplified.

Next, the drawings became abstract. Instead of representing an object, pictograms began to represent sounds called phonograms. To write "idea," using phonograms (like a rebus) you would draw the symbols for an eye and a deer. In ancient times, people used 600 symbols, and reading the writing was like unscrambling a riddle. Scribes learned to read and write in the temple school and soon became powerful people in society.

The Western alphabet comes from the Phoenicians, via the Greeks.

H.C. Rawlinson worked on an inscription engraved on a wall.

The word "hieroglyph" means "writing of the gods" in Greek. This beautiful writing of the ancient Egyptians includes both pictograms and phonograms. It has been found carved into stone in temples and tombs. Scribes also wrote in ink on scrolls of papyrus, made from reeds that grew on the banks of the Nile River. Papyrus stems were woven together, flattened, and dried to form sheets. Scribes used a quicker and more simple everyday script than hieroglyphics—demotic script. It read from right to left, as Arabic does.

Champollion grappled to uncover the secret of hieroglyphics for years, using his knowledge of other ancient languages. He succeeded, but died exhausted when he was only 42 years old.

In 1824 Jean-François Champollion, a French scientist, managed to decipher Egyptian hieroglyphics using the Rosetta Stone. The inscription carved on it was written in three ways: demotic script, hieroglyphics, and Greek. Champollion guessed it was the same text in three languages. His work has helped us learn about life in Egypt 4,000 years ago.

In 1846 Henry Rawlinson, a British diplomat, managed to decipher the cuneiform script of the Sumerians.

Each letter of the Western alphabet has its own sound. By combining the 26 letters of the Western alphabet in every possible way, a person can write down all the sounds of the Indo-European languages. Phoenician merchants invented this practical system around 1500 B.C. and used it to communicate with foreign traders. The Greeks improved the system by introducing vowels. The Romans began using the Greek alphabet and spread it throughout western Europe.

Some examples of Greek writing: it reads from left to right.

١	٢	٣	٤	٥	٦	٧	٨	٩	٠
1	7	3	8	٤	6	٦	8	9	0
1	2	3	4	5	6	7	8	9	0

How Arabic figures gradually evolved

The Greeks began writing on parchment, made of animal skins. Parchment owes its name to the town of Pergamum in present-day Turkey, where it was first made. Sheep and calf skins worked the best. They were cleaned, bleached, scraped, smoothed, and could then be used on both sides. When folded and sewn together, they made the first books in Western history, called codices.

Rolled manuscripts gave way to bound books. The Greeks introduced a new writing instrument: a reed pen, sharpened and slit down the middle to hold ink. Today's pens developed from this idea.

Writing developed further and became widely used throughout the Roman Empire. Engraved inscriptions appeared on stone monuments, praising the glory of the emperors. Scribes were often slaves. Lectors, or readers, dictated books for slaves to copy, and messengers carried written dispatches all over the Empire.

Literacy began among the privileged classes, but soon most of the Roman middle classes knew how to read and to write. The Empire was unified by a single, official language—Latin.

Numbers have a long history too. Throughout the Middle Ages, the Arabs recognized the importance of learning and traveled widely between East and West. They brought us paper, invented by the Chinese much earlier, and introduced numbers, which probably came from India. Figures started out as letters and gradually evolved into the numbers we use today. A figure's position in a number alters its value: 12 is not the same as 21, and 123 is less than 312. It's an ingenious system!

After the collapse of the Roman Empire in the fifth century, precious books were kept safe in monasteries, which had their own libraries. Here scribes, illuminators, and painters all worked together to copy the ancient manuscripts, so the knowledge they contained would not be lost.

A faster and more legible writing was developed in Emperor Charlemagne's reign in the eighth century. Carolingian script was smaller and quicker, and it looked more like today's writing. Monks and copyists wrote on parchment with pens made from goose or crow feathers, sharpened to a point. Using fine, animal-hair brushes, they painted complex designs. The colors came from gold leaf, soot, and crushed insect eggs, mixed with gelatin or egg white.

Around 1450, Gutenberg perfected the art of printing.

Movable metal type: the letters were cast in metal, and the typesetter put them together word by word, line by line.

Books were rare and expensive. It took a lot of work and a long time to copy and produce books one at a time, by hand. By the end of the Middle Ages, schools were developing; people demanded more books.

About 1447, in Mainz, Germany, Johannes Gutenberg invented a simple method to print books, using movable metal type. He arranged letters made of lead on a metal plate, covered them with ink, and pressed a sheet of paper against the metal. He repeated this until he had printed all the copies he needed.

The last stage: the printer pressed a sheet of paper against letters covered with ink.

The art of printing could never have been developed if paper had not existed. The Chinese people invented paper 2,000 years ago. They left old rags to rot in a cellar. Then they soaked and pounded the rags in huge vats of water to form a liquid pulp. They next spread the pulp on a screen, or mold, to drain and then pressed the pulp between two layers of felt, leaving the mixture to dry in the press.

Not long after Gutenberg's invention, printing workshops sprang up everywhere. Many of the workshops published Bibles and prayer books, ancient Greek and Roman works, and accounts of travels. New occupations developed: street hawkers sold books, and rag-and-bone men collected scraps of material to make into paper.

By the 19th century a large portion of the population read newspapers.

As printing methods grew faster, people began to publish single sheets of news every day. These were the first newspapers. They were called "gazettes," from the Italian *gazzetta,* the small coin that people needed to buy the paper. Gutenberg's hand-operated printing press was still used, but it could only print 300 sheets of paper a day. Soon that would not be enough.

Rotary printing presses with cylinders that turned replaced letter plates. The sheets of paper were drawn through rollers, and the ink flowed onto them automatically. But it still took too long to set the letters on the page. Then, in the 19th century, the Linotype was invented. It could set complete lines of type in strips and could typeset 9,000 characters per hour. In 1846, in the United States, the first modern printing press produced 95,000 pages of newsprint in one hour! Today, most publishing is done electronically, using computers and offset printing.

Still, even the most sophisticated machines cannot replace handwriting. Your writing is an expression of you. By writing, you can communicate in a direct and personal way with simple tools, which makes writing one of the greatest human inventions in history.

To learn to read using the Western alphabet, you have to learn 26 different letters of the alphabet. Can you read French or Spanish?

The Greek alphabet gave birth to the Cyrillic alphabet, which is used by many of the Slavonic peoples—Serbs and Russians, for example.

Arabic is one of the Semitic languages. You read it from right to left.

Indian script is about 2,000 years old. It probably developed from the Phoenician alphabet.

Chinese children have to learn thousands of different symbols, or characters. Each character is a different word.

There is no such thing as a wheel in nature. People did not just find it, as they had fire. They had to invent that round, rolling object that has become so important in so many aspects of our lives. It was an extraordinary invention, possibly the most important in human history.

Just think of life without wheels! We would not have cars, bicycles, or trains. To travel you would have to walk. To move something heavy, you would have to drag it or carry it on your back. Or, if you had a lot of help, you could fell some trees and use them like rollers to slide your load along. That is how ancient people managed to move enormous weights, like blocks of stone for building, before the invention of the wheel. Without wheels, we would have to do without all sorts of things, including clocks.

Scientists think people first made wheels in Asia Minor about 4,000 B.C. Fixed to a primitive cart, wheels helped people move substantial loads. Over the years, the heavy, solid wooden wheels developed into lighter ones with spokes. Then came the intro- duction of metal, and now our cars run on wheels protected by a cushion of air enclosed in a rubber tire!

2,500 B.C.

1,000 B.C.

Europe, 1850

Modern tire

A plow

The plow, which allowed farming to develop, was first invented without a wheel. The earliest plows, dating from about 3,500 B.C., did not have wheels but were just simple wooden blades. Wheeled plows were much more efficient. The animals did not have to strain so hard to pull them, so the furrows ran straighter and could be dug more quickly.

The plows had a metal blade, called a plowshare, which sank into the soil and dug the furrows, and an angled mouldboard, which turned the earth to one side. Soil that had been well-tilled and aired produced a good harvest. After the harvest, farmers would then take their grain to the mill. But how would the mill turn, if the wheel had not been invented?

The knife grinder sharpens knives on a grindstone.

A spinning wheel spins wool into yarn.

You turn a wheel to work the pulley on a well.

The Middle Ages saw the introduction of many machines that used multiple wheels: windmills, water mills, spinning wheels, and clocks. The movement of one wheel is transferred to another, either through a flexible link—a drive belt made of leather—or teeth called cogs, which fit into one another. These cogwheels are gears, and they can make the machine speed up or slow down.

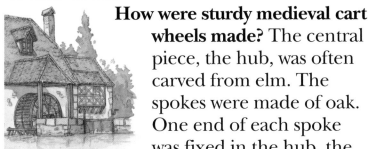

Waterwheels harnessed energy from water for paper mills, forges, tanneries, and sawmills.

How were sturdy medieval cart wheels made? The central piece, the hub, was often carved from elm. The spokes were made of oak. One end of each spoke was fixed in the hub, the other in the rim, which was made of curved pieces of wood fitted together. The outside of the rim was bound with iron to strengthen it.

Wheels can transform a jerky back-and-forth movement into a smooth, circular motion. Knife grinders, for example, pumped a foot pedal that turned the grindstone around. In forges or paper mills, wooden cams were fixed to the wheels. Each time the wheel turned, the cams lifted hammers, which in turn beat the metal or paper pulp. Even today, engines work on the principle of cranks and cams.

A treadmill can be used to lift heavy loads high in the air. One person can make it turn.

A chain pump is used to draw water. An animal turns a cogwheel, which drives another wheel fitted with buckets.

In a windmill, a system of gears transfers the movement of the sails to the grindstone, which grinds the grain into flour.

A 19th-century treadmill: a person drives the wheel around by climbing on the rungs. The rope winds up, dragging the blocks of stone along.

The heyday of the stagecoach

Stagecoaches were much faster than walking, but unfortunately, they were also dangerous. **A journey that would take you more than a week by foot could be made by stagecoach in just two days.** However, along with the driver and passengers, you would have traveled with guards who carried shotguns to fight off robbers and attackers. Harsh weather and rugged routes made travel treacherous too.

The stagecoach was suspended by leather thongs from a framework on wheels called a chassis. This suspension made the ride less bumpy and made the stagecoach easier to pull.

Between destinations, stagecoaches stopped at coach houses and horse-changing stations. Many old United States stagecoach routes were also mail routes.

From winding paths to paved roads

People in China, South America, and the Middle East built thousands of miles of roads before they ever had vehicles. After the invention of the wheel, people had to make their roads hard and straight. The Romans were the first to build networks of paved roads. Some modern roads in Europe still follow the straight lines of Roman roads. Many modern U.S. roads follow old Native American trails and wagon train routes.

Heavier vehicles needed stronger roads. In the 18th century, engineers realized that a road's foundation carries the weight of traffic, so roads need to be compressed and kept dry. If they are not, the surface becomes pitted and sunken. Roads were constructed with a curved surface so water would run off, and the base was covered with layers of small stones. In the 19th century, road-builders began to cover the surface with asphalt or concrete to make the roads smooth.

Here comes the bicycle! The first bicycle was invented in Paris in 1791. It had two wheels, but you sat on one and pushed yourself along with your feet! Later, two pedals and a crank were attached directly to the front wheel hub.

High-wheeler bicycle   Bicycle with rear chain drive   Racing bike with gears

Ten-person tandem!

The bigger the wheels, the faster the cyclist could go! Finally, the wheels were made of equal size, with the pedals placed between them with a rear chain drive. And that's how your bicycle works!

After Papin's famous steam boiler, another Frenchman, Joseph Cugnot, invented the first three-wheeled steam car in 1769.

Portable steam engines and traction engines started to replace human and animal power.

The 18th century saw a revolutionary new invention: a machine powered by steam. It was capable of pumping water, driving a hammer in a forge, and making wheels turn. The French engineer Denis Papin developed the idea of using the power of steam. Thomas Newcomen, from Great Britain, was the first to develop an efficient steam engine that was to play a major part in the Industrial Revolution.

When water boils, it turns into steam. It is possible to confine the steam in a boiler, and then let the steam escape under pressure through a valve, just as it does in a pressure cooker. This force can then be harnessed and used as energy.

The power of steam transformed life. In mines and factories people used steam to drive machinery and move heavy loads. At the beginning of the 19th century, people first attempted to run an engine on rails. Steam locomotives burned huge amounts of coal or wood, which heated a boiler full of water.

How does a steam engine move? The pressure of the steam pushes a tight-fitting metal rod, called a piston, in a cylinder. Then a valve shuts off the steam. The pressure drops, allowing the piston to come back again. The connecting rods transfer the up-and-down movement of the pistons to the wheels, and the engine moves forward.

By the beginning of the 19th century, the first steam locomotives appeared in Europe, mainly as fairground attractions. George Stephenson, a British engineer, is often called the "Father of the Railway." He built the world's first practical locomotive engine in 1825. His famous Rocket locomotive won a prize in 1829 for the best-designed steam engine. It could travel 29 mph (47 kph)—faster than a horse could gallop—which was amazing at that time.

One of the earliest trains: the carriages were simply stagecoaches set on rails. Coach makers were the first carriage makers.

A jointed connecting rod transforms the up-and-down movement of pistons into the circular movement of wheels.

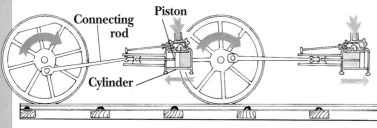

Connecting rod

Piston

Cylinder

Because the British were the first to develop a railroad system, trains all over the world drive on the left.

The first U.S. trains were imported from Great Britain. On December 25, 1830, a U.S.-built locomotive, called the "Best Friend of Charleston," carried 141 passengers in South Carolina. Soon, inventors and engineers around the country began developing new locomotive equipment and building designs.

The transcontinental railroad crossed the United States. While railways spread throughout Great Britain, the transcontinental railroad was being completed in the United States. Thousands of laborers worked in dangerous and difficult conditions to build tracks through mountains, plains, and forests. By 1869, Americans could travel from one coast to the other by train.

How is a railway track built? First the track is spread with ballast, a bed of granite chips to deaden vibration of the rails. Then the ties are laid over the top. Once they were all made of wood, but now many are made from reinforced concrete. They keep the rails firm.

The gauge is about five feet (1.4 m) in most countries. Finally, the steel rails are fixed to the ties. On an express line, they are welded together to cut down on jolts and noise.

A train's engine is powerful. It can pull all kinds of train cars, which may carry grain, automobiles, or frozen products in enormous refrigerated containers.

Steam train, around 1920

The first crossing of the U.S. by train took place in May 1869.

Many trains today run on electricity, just as streetcars and underground trains do. The power is sent through a live "third" rail, the conductor rail, where it is picked up by the train's "collector shoes." Some electric trains pick up electricity from an overhead cable and a pantograph fixed on the roof of the engine. Diesel engines are also popular today.

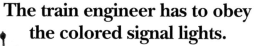

The train engineer has to obey the colored signal lights. To avoid accidents, the track is divided into sections. Once one train has started its journey onto a section, a red signal lights up and the train behind must wait until the line is clear.

Trains running through several countries cover great distances. They pull sleeping cars, dining cars, and sometimes recreation cars where children can play. About 1900 the Trans-Siberian ran from Paris to Vladivostok, a port on the far east coast of Siberia. Some of its coaches were luxurious, but if you could not afford that, you could travel third class on wooden seats. The most prestigious train of them all was the Orient Express, which crossed Europe, linking Paris with Constantinople.

In Australia you can travel 2,381 miles (3,840 km), from Perth to Sydney, on some of the straightest track in the world. People can even travel by train underneath the English Channel!

On mountainous routes, where the gradient is steepest, the rack railroad was the answer. These trains have a cogwheel that catches onto teeth in a third central rail. The highest railway in the world is in Peru, in the Andes. The rails are built in a zigzag, and the train has one engine in front and one behind.

In the 19th century, the best crafters used luxury furnishings to create carriages for important people. England's Queen Victoria enjoyed traveling by train and slept better in her sleeping car than she did in her royal palaces at Balmoral and Windsor!

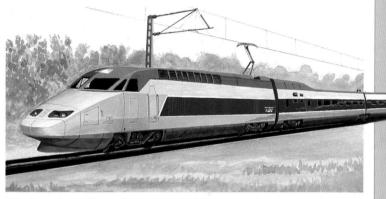

The French TGV travels at a speed of 170 mph (274 kph).

This over-ground urban train is fully automatic. It has no driver and is controlled by computer.

Marshaling yard for goods

Electric magnets keep this train—called the "Maglev"—in the air, so there is no friction on the rails. It is used in Germany and Japan.

During the first car race, between Paris and Rouen in France in July 1894, the winner reached an average speed of between 10.5 and 12.4 mph (17 and 20 kph)!

The word "auto-mobile" means "a vehicle that moves by itself." The internal combustion engine, patented in 1862, was built into a car in 1864. Karl Benz of Germany invented a three-wheeled car in 1885. By 1893 the car had four wheels, and in 1903 Henry Ford founded the Ford Motor Company. Five years later Ford produced the Model T, the first car that ordinary people could afford. Ford was able to make cars quickly and at a low cost by using a moving assembly line.

Modern trailer truck

19th century steam-powered truck

The first bus, built in 1885, carried eight passengers.

A modern bus

To fuel a steam-driven machine, people needed to carry water and wood or coal on board, but that load was cumbersome! Most modern engines are internal combustion engines. Much more practical, modern engines run on gasoline or diesel, which are both products of oil.

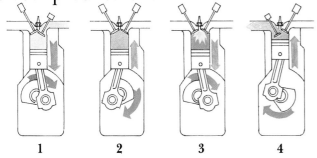

1   2   3   4

What happens inside the engine of a car?
There are four hollow tubes called cylinders. Inside each one is a piston. This is how a four-stroke engine works:
1. A piston goes down, drawing in a mixture of gasoline and air.
2. The piston goes up again, compressing the mixture.
3. The spark plug ignites a spark, which makes the gasoline explode, forcing the piston down.
4. After the explosion, a piston rises, forcing out the waste gas products.

Most engines are four-stroke engines. They have four cylinders and four spark plugs. A gasoline engine does not burn up all its fuel. It expels the waste products, including a dangerous gas called carbon monoxide, into the atmosphere.

Racing cars have wide tires. They help the car to grip the track and keep it more stable.

1854   1910   1924   1935   1990

Boats were invented thousands of years ago.

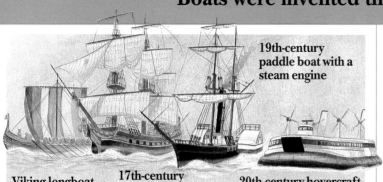

19th-century paddle boat with a steam engine

Viking longboat | 17th-century sailing ship | 20th-century hovercraft

Boats were used in Mesopotamia before 4,000 B.C. Early boats were hollowed-out tree trunks. A plank of wood served as a paddle to propel the boat. But rowing was hard work—there was no animal that

A Roman ship with a wheel rudder on the starboard side.

could be trained to do it! From ancient times up to the 16th century, slaves or prisoners were forced to wield the banks of oars on heavy ships called galleys.

On longer sea voyages, the wind's force was also used. A simple piece of cloth was hoisted to the mast to catch the wind—the sail had been invented.

The sail was a clever invention.
As the wind blows, it fills the sails and pushes the boat forward. People first made use of this discovery about 5,000 B.C. Early sails were square. Then, people living around the Mediterranean invented triangular sails: they could sail against the wind and maneuver the boat more easily.

The helm wheel turns the afterpiece of the rudder, a wide, flat piece of wood or steel.

How does a boat stay afloat? It does not sink because it is hollow, even though it is heavy. Its weight is distributed widely over the water, and a balance is maintained between the air inside the keel and the water around it.

What is a rudder? It is a flat piece of wood or metal fixed to the back, or stern, of a ship below the water. It is linked to a bar called a tiller, or a wheel. As a sailor turns the tiller to the right or to the left, the angle of the rudder moves, which causes the ship to change direction.

The great working sailing ships are long gone. Their names still have a romantic ring: barks, brigs, schooners, and clippers. Built of wood, each sturdy ship was suited to its task, such as fishing or transporting goods across the ocean.

Almost 200 years ago, the largest ships began to be built with engines instead of sails. The engine drove a paddle wheel— the paddles worked like small oars to drive the ship along. In 1836 the propeller engine was invented.

What do you think people thought of a boat built especially to go deep under the water? But that's what a submarine does!

Other giants appeared: ocean liners

At the beginning of the century, the *Mauritania's* powerful engines enabled her to cross the Atlantic in just five days. The *Titanic,* another ocean liner, claimed to be unsinkable but went down on its first voyage in 1912. These grand liners were like cities. They carried more than 1,000 passengers and hundreds of cooks, waiters, and cabin staff to look after the passengers. The last of the Atlantic liners, *Queen Elizabeth II,* was launched in 1968.

Today, only a dozen sailors are needed to handle even the largest ships. The sailors maintain radio contact with land; satellites in space keep them informed of their exact position. They use radar to locate other vessels and find out the depth of the water. An automatic pilot has taken over from a person at the helm.

A paddleboat took passengers and goods up the Mississippi River in the 19th century.

Huge propellers drive the ship forward by pushing water back. They are connected to the rudder.

Container ships

A tanker, built to carry minerals such as oil

Most ships today are built of steel.

Bird-like machines made of canvas and wood . . .

In France in 1783, the Montgolfier brothers invented the hot air balloon.

The first flying machines looked more like bats than birds! For a long time, people dreamed of flying. At the beginning of the 20th century, conquering the air seemed possible. People pursued the sport of flying enthusiastically, risking their lives in unstable contraptions made of canvas, wood, and wire.

In 1890, Clément Ader achieved the first powered takeoff. His flying machine left the ground for several feet. In 1903, the Wright brothers made the first powered flight near Kitty Hawk, North Carolina, in a small plane with propellers. In 1909, Louis Blériot crossed the English Channel from France. Then in 1927, Charles

Airships are balloons that the pilot can steer. In 1919, the Zeppelin crossed the Atlantic.

Lindbergh made the first nonstop crossing of the Atlantic in 33.5 hours, from New York to Paris.

Airplane built by the Wright brothers

Early aircraft were mostly used for carrying mail.

The Douglas "DC-3," the first modern civilian airliner, was launched in 1936. It could carry 21 passengers. Twenty years later, airliners had developed into giants like the Boeing 707, which can carry as many as 184 passengers.

There's a highway code in the air as well as on the road! To avoid accidents, aircraft travel in air corridors, which are like invisible lanes in the sky. If two aircraft are using the same corridor, they have to leave a certain amount of space between them. Before takeoff, the pilots make a flight plan: they choose the route they will follow based on weather reports, the distance, and the altitude of the flight. Radio and radar track all aircraft from the ground.

Clément Ader's first flight

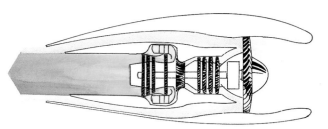

By shooting the air out from behind, the turbofan propels the aircraft forward.

How does an airplane fly? Its speed and the shape of its wings keep it in the air. The air flowing over the top of the wing travels faster than the air flowing underneath. This causes a difference in pressure above and below the wing and gives the plane lift. At takeoff, the pilot turns the wings into the wind to give the plane added lift.

Although the planes are big, they have to be light, so they are often built of aluminum. Until the 1950s, aircraft were fitted with combustion engines (like cars), which drove propellers, but the fastest they could fly was 434 mph (700 kph). Today they are built with turbojets.

Jet aircraft have powerful engines. The turbojet draws in the cold air, heats it up by burning fuel, then shoots it out from the back at enormous speed. This leaves the white vapor trail seen in the sky.

The Canari bird, 1929

Boeing 727

AIR FRANCE

Ultralight

Helicopter

Light airplane with propellers

Jet aircraft need a long runway for takeoff and landing. Some airports are too small for jets, but can handle light aircraft. Small planes and those with propellers still perform a valuable service in many parts of the world, especially where few roads exist.

Instead of wings, helicopters have blades that spin at a high speed. They rarely travel faster than 186 mph (300 kph), but they can land almost anywhere: on a mountain, in a clearing, or on the roof of a building.

Helicopters can fly very low and even hover. They are used for keeping an eye on roads and forests, for transporting injured people quickly to hospitals, and as luxury taxis for those wealthy enough to afford them!

Measuring the world

It was only two centuries ago that people learned how to measure long distances and pinpoint precise positions around the globe. Complicated instruments and difficult mathematics are needed to make these calculations with accuracy.

How to find out where on Earth you are! As Earth rotates, different countries receive the sun's light, one after another. When the sun rises in Europe, it is night in North America and midday in India.

To measure speed, sailors used a knotted rope trailing behind the boat. They counted knots as sand ran through the hourglass.

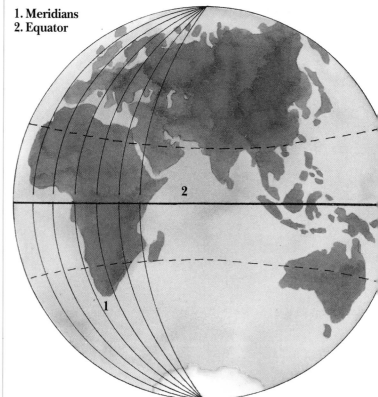

1. Meridians
2. Equator

The meridians are imaginary lines around Earth, connecting the North Pole to the South Pole.

Scientists divide the world into time zones marked out by the meridians. The most famous meridian, the Greenwich Meridian, passes through London, England. To work out their position at sea, sailors calculate the longitude and latitude, which is their position east or west of the Greenwich Meridian and north or south of the equator—another imaginary line circling Earth halfway between the two poles. To find out latitude, navigators measure the angle between the sun and the horizon—since the angle varies according to where a person is on Earth, he or she can get an accurate position.

An astronomical clock shows the movement of the planets.

Telling the passing hours

The nocturlabe, like the astrolabe, is an old-fashioned instrument that tells the time by measuring the height of the stars above the horizon.

Our ancestors used to measure time by the passing of the seasons and by the rising, progression, and setting of the sun. By observing stars in the night sky, astronomers in ancient times divided the day into 12 hours and the year into 360 days. We now know that it takes Earth 24 hours to make a complete turn on its axis, and 365 days and six hours to make a full circuit of the sun.

To make up those extra six hours into a full day, we have 366 days in every fourth, or leap, year.

For sports competitions, a stopwatch can measure time to 0.01 of a second.

What time is it? People in the ancient world used to tell the time with sundials, sand timers, and water clocks. The first mechanical clocks were invented in the Middle Ages; the regular swinging of a weight on the end of a pendulum turned the hands. Later, a spring that slowly unwound replaced the pendulum. When you wind a watch or clock, you wind up the spring again.

Quartz clocks and watches use an electric battery that sets a quartz crystal vibrating. Atomic clocks are so accurate that they only lose one second every 3,000 years! They are used to set the international standard for a second.

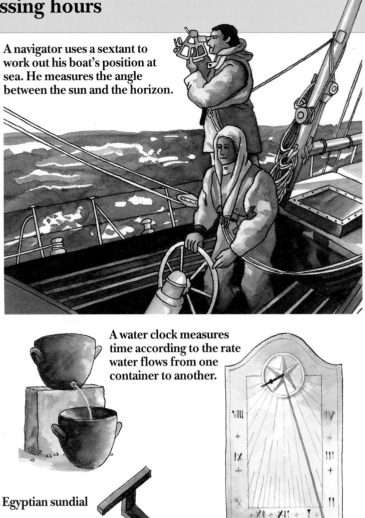

A navigator uses a sextant to work out his boat's position at sea. He measures the angle between the sun and the horizon.

A water clock measures time according to the rate water flows from one container to another.

Egyptian sundial

The shadow cast by the gnomon on a sundial points to the hour of the day.

A sand timer

A watch and its mechanism

The invention of the spring allowed small watches to be built; people could carry them in their pocket or on their wrist.

These clocks have weights and a pendulum: the pendulum regulates the mechanism, and the weights control the pendulum.

Think of all the things you do when you get up in the morning. You get out of bed, turn on the light, wash, make and eat breakfast, and go to school by foot, bus, bike, or car. From the moment you open your eyes you use electricity, gas, oil . . . and your own muscles. You use energy all the time!

Energy comes from the Greek word *energeia,* which means "power in action." A body or a system has energy if it is capable of doing work, or in other words, transferring power.

When a horse uses its strength to pull a plow, it is working and using energy. When you pedal your bike to make it go fast, you use some of the energy you stored up when you had breakfast. Every second of the day people use energy.

The search for sources of energy, as well as ways to conserve the energy we already have, is one of the most important concerns of our modern society.

There are many different forms of energy, such as: mechanical, electrical, chemical, thermal, and nuclear. You can transform one form of energy into another. A battery transforms chemical energy into electrical energy, and a steam engine transforms thermal energy into mechanical energy.

All these harness, produce, or transform energy:
1. Dam 2. Solar panels 3. Uranium mine
4. Nuclear power station 5. Windmill
6. Hydroelectric power station built on a river (using the energy produced by water) 7. Coal mine 8. Tidal power station
9. Oil rig 10. Oil refinery 11. Power plant making gas from coal
12. Forestry 13. Organic farm waste used to produce methane gas
14. House with solar panels

People did not master electricity until the 19th century.

Before houses had electricity, people used individual lamps, lit by candles, oil, or gas.

Electricity: it is so easy for us to use that we take it for granted.

Obtaining light or heat at the flick of a switch would have seemed like magic to our ancestors. Even so, we know that the first experiments with electricity were made a long time ago. About 2,500 years ago, the Greek philosopher and scientist Thales of Miletus found he could cause sparks if he rubbed some amber with a piece of cloth. Thales had discovered static electricity. But it was many centuries before anyone discovered how to produce and make use of an electric current or generator.

In 1800 Alessandro Volta demonstrated his electric battery to a group of scientists. The French emperor Napoleon (seated at the table) was also present.

What makes electricity work?

When an electric current passes along a wire, millions of minute particles called electrons move about, colliding with the atoms that make up the metallic wire. As the atoms are disturbed, they release energy in the form of heat or light. The quantity of heat or light produced is proportional to the resistance of the conducting wire. In other words, the more the atoms resist as the electrons move along, the greater the heat that is produced.

Certain things, like wood or glass, do not conduct electricity at all. Others, like iron and many other metals, are conductors, but they are resistant. The filament in an electric light bulb works on this principle. It is made of tungsten, a metal that offers great resistance, so it gets hotter and hotter until it glows and produces light.

Volta's battery

Electricity: magic for everyone!

Thomas Edison lit up the world when he invented the electric light. You can read on a light bulb how powerful it is. A 100-watt bulb is brighter than one of 25 watts. In the United States, household appliances run on 220 volts. Volts are the electrical pressure that pushes an electric current around a circuit. The name comes from the Italian physicist Alessandro Volta, who invented the first electric battery in 1794.

Thomas Edison invented the first electric light bulb. The lack of oxygen in the bulb allows the wire filament to heat up and glow white hot without burning.

The first battery

Volta's battery was made from a series of silver discs separated from one another by wads of cloth soaked in salt water. Today, batteries aren't quite so big! Some of them are smaller than a pea.

You can produce electricity yourself!

Some bike lights work without a battery. As the biker pedals, a generator attached to the wheel transforms the person's energy into electric energy and produces a current to power the light. Inside the generator is a magnet and an electric circuit, connected to the wheel as it turns.

Car batteries are storage batteries; as the car engine moves, it recharges the battery.

Providing electricity for a whole country

During the last century, coal powered electric power stations. As the coal burned, it heated water, which turned into steam. The steam was used to drive turbines that generated electricity . . . just like the generator on some bike lights.

In 1882, Edison lit up the city of New York with electric light from his coal-fired electric power station.

Fossil fuels: coal and oil

During the 19th century, cities in Europe and the United States became industrialized and used coal as the main source of energy. It was used in many different ways: to drive steam engines, to produce electricity, and to smelt iron for the steel needed for building machines.

What is coal? Coal, a fossil, is formed from the remains of trees and giant ferns that grew on Earth about 250 million years ago. Away from the air, the vegetation of rivers and swamps rotted and gradually turned into carbon.

There are different types of coal. Those compressed the longest, such as anthracite, are rich in carbon and are the better quality coals. Lignite and peat are softer and contain less carbon, and they do not burn as well.

Where is coal found? Since the Middle Ages, people have mined coal in open-cast mines. Later, they learned how to dig tunnels deep into the earth, looking for seams of coal. Mining has always been dangerous, laborious work.

About one-third of the world's coal mines are located in the United States.

Petroleum: an underground treasure

Today, stocks of coal in many pits have been exhausted; others are too expensive to mine and have been closed down.

Petroleum has replaced coal for many uses. The name "petroleum" means "oil from rock"—it looks like a thick greenish-brown liquid, and it springs out of the ground. Petroleum's other name is crude oil. Like coal, it is formed from organic material. Over millions of years, plants and animals died and drifted to the sea bottom. Layers of soil gathered over the sludge, and pockets of it were trapped between layers of rock. Time and heat from pressure turned the sludge into oil.

Deep wells are dug to extract oil from under the ground. The first commercial oil field was opened in 1859 in Pennsylvania. Some countries do not have their own oil fields and import their petroleum—it can travel great distances.

First, oil is transported in huge pipes to the sea . . .

. . . where it is loaded onto giant oil tankers . . .

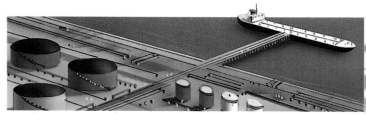

. . . that take it to large industrial ports.

Gas and water drive power stations.

High tension cables (400,000 volts) carry electricity from the power stations to the cities where it is needed.

Other sources of energy from underground

Butane and propane gas are present in the subsoil. We call them natural gases to distinguish them from industrial gases. Because natural gases burn, people most often use them for heating and cooking, but gases can be used for lighting as well, such as neon and krypton. Like oil, gases are transported in giant pipelines.

A clean form of energy

Water power can also produce electricity. The force of the water as it spills from the top of a dam is used to drive turbines.

Petroleum is purified in huge oil refineries and made ready for its different uses.

Tanker trucks transport it to a point of sale . . .

. . . a gas station, for example.

They are then divided into lower tension cables (11,000 volts), which carry the electricity to individual houses at between 120 and 240 volts.

Some environmentalists urge governments to make more use of water power, which is cleaner and more abundant than oil and a better use of Earth's resources.

A dam

What is nuclear energy?

An atom: electrons spinning around a central nucleus

The industrialized nations of the world demand more and more energy. Every 10 years, we double the amount of electricity we use. In the United States today, nuclear power stations produce about 25 percent of the electricity.

The heart of the matter

"Nuclear" comes from the Latin word "nucleus," meaning core. All matter is made up of atoms, each with a nucleus. To produce energy, nuclear power stations use atoms from metals such as uranium-235 and plutonium. Splitting the nuclei of these atoms into two produces a great heat. This heat brings water to the boiling point, and the steam drives turbines, just as in a coal-fired power station. But one gram of uranium-235 produces as much energy as two or three tons of coal! It is by far the most concentrated source of energy used by humans.

Symbol warning danger from nuclear radiation

Nuclear energy has dangers

As the uranium and plutonium create nuclear power, they produce radioactive waste: the waste products contain dangerous rays. These radioactive rays can harm or kill living things. Nuclear waste can remain dangerous for thousands or even billions of years, so what can we do with it?

If we continue to dump it underground, are we just storing the problem for the future? Some people believe that it may be better to keep the waste in specially designed containers and buildings above ground, so that scientists can check them regularly. Others believe that we should use safer forms of energy.

Cutaway diagram of a nuclear reactor: on the left (red) is the atomic pile, which heats the water of the primary circuit (orange). The primary circuit heats the water in the secondary circuit (yellow), turning it to steam. The steam drives an alternator that produces electricity.

The sun: a source of energy that can never be used up

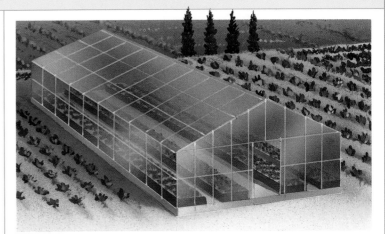

Clean energy, green power

We could make better use of the forces of nature to provide energy in ways less harmful to the environment. We do not have to use up irreplaceable resources. We can harness the power of the wind with windmill "farms" to produce electricity. In certain parts of the world, natural hot springs of water or steam, called geysers, jet up into the air. In Iceland, geysers supply domestic heating and enable people to grow a variety of fruits and vegetables, even though the weather is very cold.

Solar energy

In northern climates during the cold winter months, farmers can grow vegetables in greenhouses, where large panes of glass let in plenty of sunlight. Sunlight warms the soil, which absorbs and then reemits infrared rays. The glass traps the rays, which in turn keep the temperature inside the greenhouse warm. If Earth only received a tiny amount of the sun's rays, this part would still represent 10,000 times more energy than we need. But how do we collect and use the energy?

Sunlight powers this telephone.

Today, solar power gives us heat. Some people use the sun's rays to heat their homes in the same way as others use the rays for greenhouses. Solar collectors on dark, heat-absorbent metallic plates heat up just like the soil in a greenhouse does. The trapped heat either warms the air directly, or heats a circuit of water that feeds the radiators—solar central heating!

Solar power turned into electricity

The sun's light energy can also be turned directly into electricity using photovoltaic cells, as some European industries do. Sunlight can also be used to make steam, which can power a turbine and produce electricity. A solar energy plant in California does this by collecting sunlight with a tower of mirrors.

A house with solar heating is fitted with panels of photoelectric cells. Sloping panels can receive more solar energy than vertical ones.

Did you know that light is made up of colors?

Isaac Newton passed a light through a prism and found that white sunlight breaks down into different colored lights.

Light that reaches us from the sun appears transparent and is known as white light. In fact, it is a combination of an infinite number of colored lights. In 1666, the English physicist Isaac Newton made sunlight pass through a prism—a small glass pyramid—and showed that white light is made up of the seven colors of the rainbow.

In fact, there are many more than seven colors between violet and red, and many others cannot be seen by the human eye.

Before electric light, people used candles made of animal fat or wax. The light the candles shed was weak and orange-colored.

In the triangle are the three primary colors. Around the circle are the three complementary colors, made from mixing two primary colors.

Light is a wave. When light hits anything that is not transparent, part of it is absorbed and part of it is reflected. If we think an object is yellow, it's because that object reflects the yellow light and absorbs the other colors. If it looks red, it's because it is only reflecting red light.

This discovery led scientists to believe that light is made up of waves, rather like ripples on the surface of water. The color waves vary in shape—some are sharper than others. Red has the lowest pitch and the longest wavelength, and violet has the highest pitch and the shortest wavelength.

Heat is the source of light. When any substance is heated, it glows and becomes luminous once its temperature has reached 932° Fahrenheit (500°C). As its temperature rises to 1,832°F (1,000°C), its color gradually changes from deep red to a red that is almost white. Until Thomas Edison invented the electric light bulb in 1880, people did not have bright light. They only knew the gentle glow from burning oil and resin—candles made of animal fat or wax—then later, alcohol or gas lamps.

The filament, or thread, in early electric light bulbs was heated to 5,072°F (2,800°C) by an electric current. Today, the filament in a halogen lamp reaches 7,232°F (4,000°C). It can stand such a high temperature because it is bathed in a gas called halogen. Glass would shatter at this heat, so the bulb itself is made of quartz.

Colored lights from burning powders

Certain powders can color flames. The color of a light does not always depend on the temperature of the thing that is burning. For example, if someone threw certain powdered substances into the flame of a blowtorch, the substances would glow brightly and color the flames for a moment.

The art of making fireworks is called pyrotechnics. A firework is made of two cartridges. One is filled with gunpowder to launch the rocket into the air and light the other cartridge—the one that produces brilliant flames of different colors. This second cartridge is filled with a mixture of substances that burn and different powders: zinc and copper powder for the blues and greens, sodium for the yellows, and so on.

Fireworks must always be used with great care. They provide a spectacular display for a celebration such as the Fourth of July!

Moving pictures: the birth of cinema!

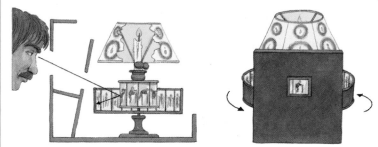

A praxinoscope: images reflect off of mirrors and seem to move.

Photography, cinema, and television are part of our daily lives. They have all been invented since the early 19th century, and each one makes use of light.

The birth of photography
Certain substances, such as silver chloride and Judean bitumen, turn solid black under the effect of light.

People had realized this for a long time, but it was in 1827 that the French physicist Nicephore Niepce put the knowledge to work and produced photographs. He covered a pewter plate with bitumen and exposed it in a camera. Where light fell on it, the bitumen turned hard and black. Softer areas were then washed away, leaving a well-defined image.

This process was perfected in 1838 by Niepce's associate, Jacques Daguerre. His photographic images, known as daguerreotypes, soon became popular for portraits. In 1859, the British physicist James Maxwell took the world's very first color photograph.

The way was opened to cinematography. Since 1852, scientists have been able to break down movement photographically into a sequence of still images. Many years before the cinema, people knew how to project these images through the "magic lantern." Then instruments like the praxinoscope made it possible to put the movement back together again.

When images are shown rapidly enough one after another, a person's eyes hold the image he or she has just seen for a fraction of a second, even though the following image has already appeared. This is the principle of animation. The Lumière brothers put all these inventions together and gave us the cinema. They held their first public viewing in 1895.

Pictures you see on television consist of tiny points of light that move about on the screen. The closer together the points of light, the more clear-cut the image; and the more quickly that they move about, the steadier the picture. The pictures on TV come from patterns of light that arrange and rearrange themselves 50 times a second! All variations of color come from different combinations of just three series of luminous dots: red, blue, and green.

What is a laser beam? Lasers are made from pure, concentrated light. They emit beams so intense that they can travel great distances without growing dim or fading away. Astronomers direct beams onto small mirrors placed on the Moon and then wait for them to "bounce back." Light travels at a certain speed, so scientists know that Earth is 238,860 miles (384,326 km) away! Even greater distances can be calculated in light years, or the distance light travels in one year.

Printers use lasers to reproduce full-color pictures. The scanner's photoelectric eye moves over a picture to analyze it. It sorts out the colors and relays information to the laser so that color film can be produced for the printer.

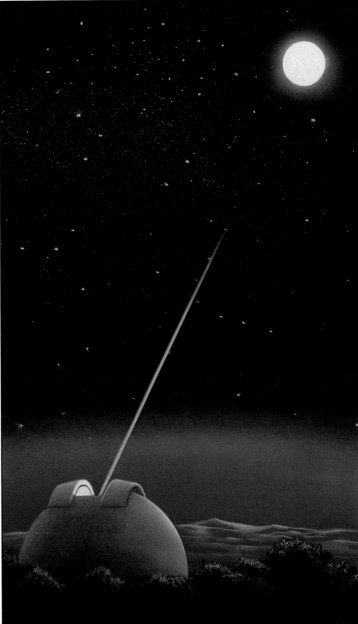

The pictures you see in this book are all made up of just four colors: black, blue (cyan), red (magenta), and yellow, each reproduced on a plate. When the printer puts the four images on top of one another, they form pictures like those in this book.

Sputnik, the first artificial satellite, launched in 1957

If you travel a distance of 50 miles (80 km) into the sky, you will find yourself in the emptiness of space, far above the atmosphere where you are able to breathe.

Before space travel was possible, rockets—which can reach 17,390 mph (28,000 Kph) —had to be invented.

A hundred years after author Jules Verne wrote about a cannon-ball rocket, the huge Saturn V sent spacecraft to the Moon.

A rocket needs no air: it takes its own oxygen supply to burn its fuel. The thrust of the first few minutes carries the rocket rapidly up into space.

In Massachusetts in 1926, Robert Goddard launched the first rocket.

"That's one small step for man, one giant leap for mankind."

So much preparation goes into sending astronauts into space. It takes years! Scientists must build a spaceship with everything the passengers will need for their journey: air, water, food, and fuel. The spaceship must be capable of returning to Earth later.

To leave its orbit and reenter Earth's atmosphere, the spaceship brakes, then uses the air's friction to slow its speed from 17,390 mph (28,000 kph) to zero! One tiny error, and the spaceship will burn up.

The Soviet astronaut Yuri Gagarin was the first human to orbit Earth. It took 108 minutes on April 12, 1961. John Glenn was the first American astronaut. He completed an orbit in February 1962.

Landing on the Moon

To reach the Moon, a spacecraft needs to move at a speed of 24,800 mph (40,000 kph) as it leaves Earth, and travel about 2.5 million miles (4 million km).

In 1957 a Russian dog named Laika was the first living creature to travel in space.

Landing on the Moon, which has no atmosphere, had to be done gently, using rocket engines, not parachutes. Then the whole procedure had to be carried out in reverse to take off again from the moon.

On May 25, 1961, President John F. Kennedy challenged scientists to develop space technology: "America will land a man on the Moon before 1970," he said. The challenge was met: on July 20, 1969, Neil Armstrong and Edwin Aldrin walked on the Moon's surface. That walk was the climax of one of the greatest enterprises of all time: the Apollo space project. The National Aeronautics and Space Administration (NASA) built a giant rocket, Saturn V, and a spacecraft capable of landing on the Moon, the Apollo lunar module.

The Apollo command module splashed down in the Pacific Ocean on its return to Earth.

The astronauts used a lunar roving vehicle to travel on the Moon's surface.

The Apollo lunar module

Communication satellites handle all kinds of electronic communications in the form of microwaves. These are telephone calls, radio and television broadcasts, and fax messages.

The first satellite, Sputnik, was sent into space on October 4, 1957, powered by the Soviet rocket Zemiorka. The space age had begun. The first American satellite, called Explorer, was launched on January 31, 1958.

Exploring the Moon and traveling through space provides us with important new knowledge. High above Earth, in the airless world of space, hundreds of artificial moons, or satellites, circle silently in orbit. They explore an environment that was unknown until now.

From their orbits, satellites can pick up clear signals from the stars (such as gamma rays, X and ultraviolet rays, visible and infrared light, and radio waves) before they are distorted by Earth's atmosphere.

Modern telephones link up through space! Communication satellites, comsats, make it possible for information to travel from one end of the world to the other on super-high-frequency radio waves called microwaves. This is how we can communicate instantly over vast distances.

Satellites don't need engines. Although it moves through space at 17,390 mph (28,000 kph) or more, a satellite has no engine. Just as Earth moves around the Sun, or the Moon around Earth, satellites circle—or orbit—our planet continuously.

NASA's space shuttle

Observatories in space have revolutionized astronomy.

Now it is possible to watch the birth and death of a star, probe the heart of the galaxies, and look at quasars, the objects farthest away from us in space. The most important astronomical satellite, the Hubble Space Telescope, was sent into orbit in 1990. Astronomers can point it in any direction to photograph distant objects that we cannot see well through telescopes on Earth.

Earth seen from the cosmos

Geostationary satellites move at a certain speed so that they remain always over the same point on the Earth's surface. They look at the formation and breakup of clouds, for example. This type of satellite takes the "satellite pictures" seen on TV weather forecasts.

Earth survey satellites are not so far away.

They are in orbit at about 434 to 620 miles (700 to 1,000 km) above Earth and study fields, forests, coasts, and houses. Spot, a well-known French satellite, takes less than one month to pass over every part of the Earth. The pictures it sends back are detailed enough to show the dimensions of a truck!

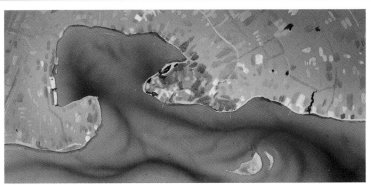

We can look at coastlines and detect pollution from pictures sent to Earth from a satellite.

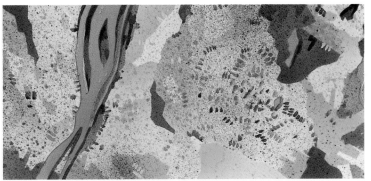

Satellite photographs can be false-colored to give scientists a geological map of an area.

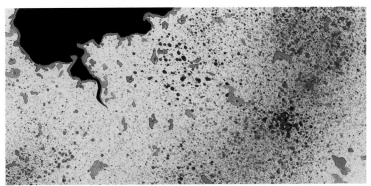

Earth survey satellites let us predict harvests, monitor the health of forests, and get lots of ecological and agricultural information.

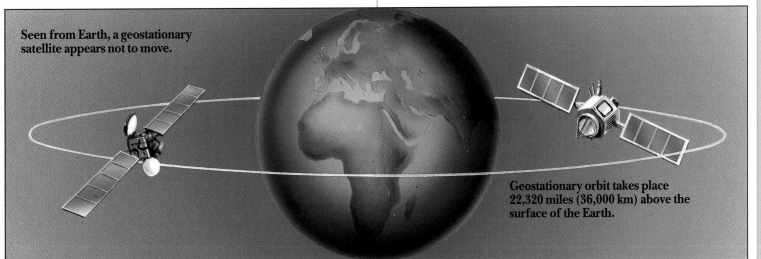

Seen from Earth, a geostationary satellite appears not to move.

Geostationary orbit takes place 22,320 miles (36,000 km) above the surface of the Earth.

Will it be possible to build a city in space?

Ariane and Hermes: Europeans in space

The United States and the former Soviet Union took the world into the space age. Other countries now have space programs too. Soon, European astronauts will leave Earth in a spaceship called Hermes, launched by the rocket Ariane V. They will work on an all-European space station, Columbus. When it is finished, Columbus will join other space stations already orbiting in space.

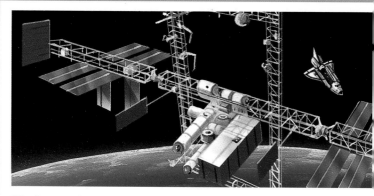

The international space station Freedom will be put together from hundreds of small pieces.

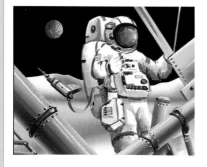

Space stations are growing larger all the time! The first ones, launched in the 1970s, were about the size of a semitrailer.

The Russian station Mir, which means peace, now looks more like an entire train. Since it was launched in 1986, astronauts have added onto and rearranged it—all the work was done in space! Between two and six people live there for periods ranging from one month to a whole year.

Living in space . . .

Engineers are now working on the space station Freedom. This international project includes two American modules, one European (Columbus), and one Japanese. In the 21st century, these stations may develop into space colonies, where thousands of people could live.

Return to the Moon . . .

Astronauts will probably go back to the Moon at the beginning of the 21st century. This time, it won't be just a flying visit. Humans will be there to stay. A permanent base could be set up for the Moon to become a scientific observatory. People could use materials from the Moon to develop industry in space. The new space factories, as well as people on Earth, could use solar energy, of which there is a limitless supply in space and on the Moon.

Objective: Mars!

The biggest aim of our adventures in space is the famous red planet, Mars. Is there, or has there ever been, life on Mars? We already know that the climate there is very dry and cold. But Mars has not always been a frozen desert. Rivers once flowed, and it still has mounds of ice. Perhaps there is water deep underground!

The spacecraft Pathfinder, which landed on Mars July 4, 1997, has provided valuable information. It will probably be in your lifetime that astronauts first set foot on the red planet. Ahead are new challenges for humans. The cosmos will be opened up to discovery, and who knows what inventions lie in store!

The first astronauts to arrive on Mars might stay there several months. Although they will reach the red planet in a large spaceship, they will probably land on it in a small capsule.

Some scientists think that one day people will travel to the Moon again—and this time they'll stay to live and work.

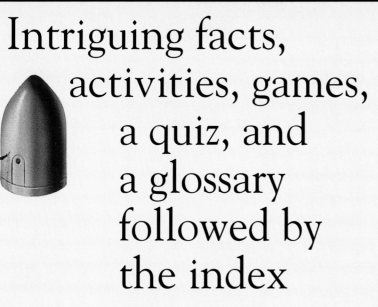

Intriguing facts, activities, games, a quiz, and a glossary followed by the index

■ Did you know?

Traveling and measuring

The wish to travel faster and farther led to the invention of the rudder, the wheel, the steam engine, and electricity. Using these, people could explore the world and conquer new lands.

A wheel dating from 2000 B.C.

This map shows the world as Europeans knew it around 1600. They had yet to explore Greenland and northern Asia, and had not traveled into the heart of North America. From the end of the 15th century, Spanish ships regularly crossed the Atlantic, and the Portuguese rounded the southern tip of Africa on their route to India and the exotic Spice Islands. Gradually, they established colonies in these new countries, first on the coasts and then farther and farther inland. From these distant lands merchants acquired exotic goods: silk, spices, perfumes, cotton, sugarcane, cocoa beans, and thousands of other valuable things.

In the 17th century, the British and the Dutch began to open trade routes overseas. In 1600, Queen Elizabeth I chartered the famous East India Company, which ruled trade between England and the Far East.

In 1607, the first colony was established in North America, at Jamestown, Virginia. In 1620, the Mayflower landed at Plymouth Rock, in what later became Massachusetts.

Map of the world around 1600

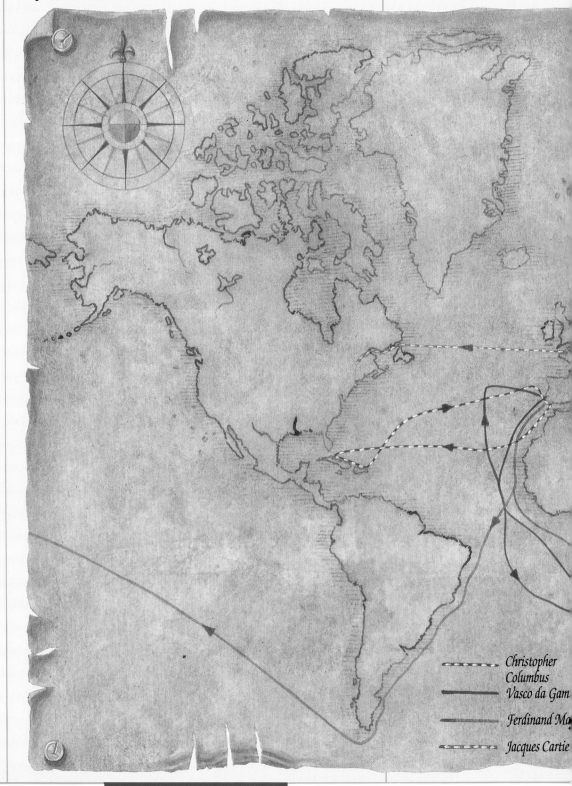

Christopher Columbus

Vasco da Gam

Ferdinand Ma

Jacques Cartie

What is speed? It is the relationship between a distance and the time taken to cover that distance. Speed is usually calculated in miles per hour in the United States. Most other countries use kilometers per hour.

Sailors used to figure out the speed of a ship by using a rope with knots tied in it at regular intervals. We say a boat is traveling at 10 knots when it has traveled 10 nautical miles in one hour. One nautical mile is equal to 1.2 miles (1.9 km)

When there is a storm raging, how hard is the wind blowing? An anemometer measures wind speed. There is also the Beaufort scale (from 0 to 12), worked out by Francis Beaufort. A fresh breeze would be Force 4, but bad weather's coming if it rises to Force 8 or 9.

Some cars can travel at speeds of 185 mph (300 kph), but a huge aircraft called the Concorde can travel faster than the speed of sound. Called Mach speed, the speed of sound is about 742 mph (1,194 kph).

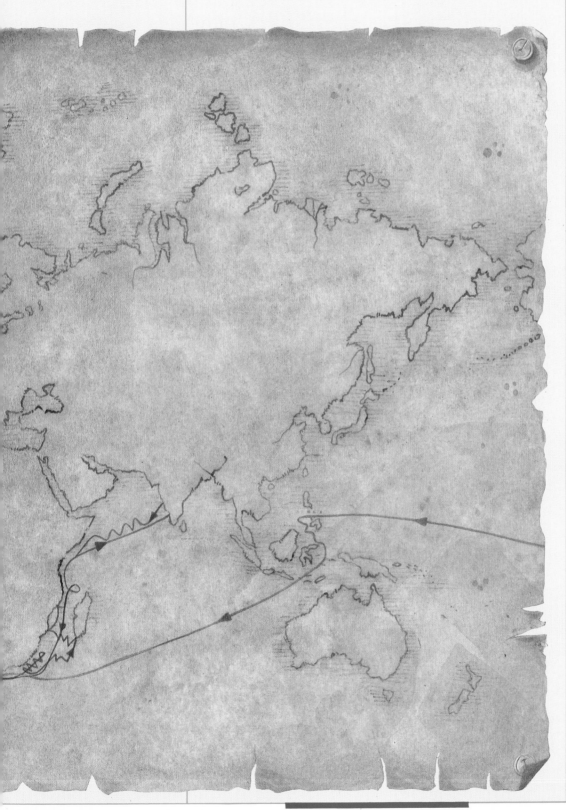

Sunshine and rain
Measuring cold, heat, dryness, and humidity and forecasting variations in our climate are all part of the science of meteorology. Meteorologists use sophisticated instruments like geostationary satellites. Forecasting the weather may simply be interesting for many of us, but for sailors, aircraft pilots, and farmers, the information may be of vital importance.

Thermometers
The centigrade, or Celsius scale, takes the freezing point of water as 0°C, and the boiling point as 100°C. On the Fahrenheit scale, water freezes at 32°F and boils at 212°F. Thermometers show the temperature by means of mercury or alcohol, which expands or contracts inside a glass tube as it gets hotter or colder.

Barometers show changes in air pressure,
which is measured in millibars. Air pressure changes affect the weather. The needle on a barometer moves as the pressure in the atmosphere changes. In 1643 the Italian physicist Evangelista Torricelli invented the mercury barometer.

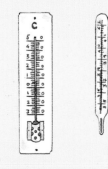

■ Did you know?

Canals are not natural waterways. Some form a link between two seas or two regions, and some help with irrigation, bringing water to areas where it is in short supply. The level of a canal must remain even all along its length. This may mean digging through hills and building aqueducts across valleys. If the land is too uneven, locks have to be built between levels.

Why do trains travel on the left? Long before the railroad was invented, English knights who met on horseback in a narrow lane would each keep to the left, so their swords would not clash. Since the first railroad engineers were British, the practice was adopted in most parts of the world, even though in most countries road users drive on the right.

The canal at Corinth, in Greece, links the Aegean Sea with the Ionian Sea. This enormous cutting took 10 years to complete.

A boat drives into a lock, and the gates close behind it.

The sluice gates open, and water flows into the lock chamber.

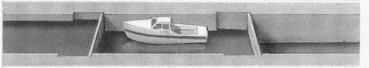

When the water level has risen to the same level as outside the lock, the gates open and the boat moves through.

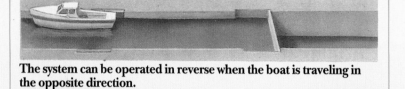

The system can be operated in reverse when the boat is traveling in the opposite direction.

The wheels of the future will turn in space. They won't roll along roads but will guide spacecraft and satellites observing Earth and taking photographs while in orbit.

Electromagnets make the wheel in a satellite turn quickly, because they cut down on friction and wear and tear. This also means there is less risk of a breakdown. As the wheel speeds up or slows down, the satellite changes direction.

Space airplane Hermes transported by an Airbus

Hermes in flight

Rocket Ariane

Did you know?

Daily life, daily pleasures

Clothes are a human invention too! Prehistoric tribespeople used needles made of bone to sew skins together with animal sinews. The first metal needles didn't appear until around 3,000 B.C.

By that time, the Chinese already know how to weave silk thread produced by caterpillars, and the Egyptians gathered hemp to make into tunics. We don't know who invented spinning and weaving. Both take a long time and need skill and patience.

For many hundreds of years, it was the women's task to make the clothes that their families wore. Only the rich could afford to go to tailors and dressmakers.

The first sewing machines appeared in 1830. They were used to make military uniforms.

Music has not always been written down in the same way. From top to bottom: musical score from the 15th century, score from the 20th century, and modern notation, which is evolving due to modern electronic instruments

Where did music and musical instruments come from? Music, song, and dance seem to have been part of ceremony and celebration since the earliest times. The first musical instruments were made out of objects that were in everyday use: an earthenware pot covered with an animal skin made a drum, and a reed pierced with holes became a flute.

Up until the Middle Ages, people learned songs by hearing them repeated. There was no way of writing down the notes. But then music began to grow more complicated, and if people were going to be able to remember it, they had to find a way of writing it down. A Benedictine monk had the idea of inscribing signs on a stave of four lines, to show the pitch of each note and how long it should be held. Gradually, the system was improved, and musicians composed pieces for many different instruments.

The first public concerts were held in the 17th century. Before then, orchestras only played in the royal courts of kings and princes.

Who taught you to play?
No one! All babies play with anything they can get ahold of. Play is a way of learning about the world and gaining skills. As babies grow older, they play with more complicated toys.

Many of the games we play have their roots in the past. In the Middle Ages, children played hide-and-seek and blindman's bluff, as well as charades and dances with actions, like nursery rhymes. People also played checkers and chess, and they invented a variety of card games.

Made from cloth, wood, or china, dolls have existed for as long as there have been children, but the first teddy bears were made in 1900.

■ Quiz

Try to answer these questions. The answers are at the bottom of the page.

1. In which country was the compass invented?
a. China
b. India
c. Portugal

2. Windmills first appeared in Europe in
a. Roman times.
b. the Middle Ages.
c. the 19th century.

3. The Western way of writing stems from the
a. Egyptians.
b. Sumerians.
c. Americans.

4. One of the ships Christopher Columbus used to cross the Atlantic was named the
a. Santa Maria.
b. Santa Barbara.
c. Hermione the Great.

5. The first living creature to be sent into space was a
a. monkey.
b. rabbit.
c. dog.

6. The highest railway is in
a. France.
b. Germany.
c. Peru.

7. The first man to walk on the Moon was
a. Yuri Gagarin.
b. Neil Armstrong.
c. John Kennedy.

Answers
1a, 2b, 3b, 4a, 5c, 6c, 7b

Would you like to play a game with these fierce pirates?

Help them open the door of their cave. First, you need to discover the password. Figure it out from the letters printed in heavy type on the rocks. Then find the key that fits the keyhole.

What is hidden behind these rocks? A fabulous animal?

A poor prisoner?

Coffers full of gold doubloons?

Sapphires and rubies?

Rivers of diamonds?

The password is "treasure." The right key is no. 7.

66

■ True or false?

1. Champollion was a great archaeologist who discovered temples in ancient Greece.

2. The first text that Gutenberg printed, in about 1450, was a newspaper.

3. The inventor of the phonograph, an early record player, was deaf.

4. Satellites don't need engines to orbit Earth.

5. Peat is the highest quality of coal.

6. The battery was invented by Alessandro Volta.

7. People have no real uses for laser beams.

You might hear expressions connected with measuring. Have you heard these? "For good measure" means something extra added to what is due.

If something is "made to measure," it fits well and suits a person perfectly.

"Give him an inch, and he'll take a mile" means he will take advantage of you, given the chance.

Milestones were set along a road to mark off each mile; now the expression means a significant event or stage in your life.

■ Games

Make your own cartoon: Happy Man, Sad Man. Take a long, thin piece of paper and fold it in the middle.

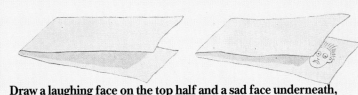

Draw a laughing face on the top half and a sad face underneath, toward the end farthest from the fold.

Roll the top part round a pencil, then move the pencil to left and right quickly; your small person won't know whether to laugh or cry!

A flicker book

Take a pad of paper and draw an animal in the bottom right-hand corner of the last page, then draw it moving very slightly on each page till you get to the top.

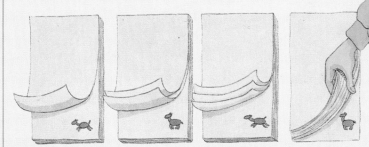

As you flick the pages, your animal will skip and run!

Topsy-turvy

You need a small cardboard circle, two pieces of string, and a pen. On one side of the disc, draw a dog with his mouth open; on the other side of the disc, draw him with his mouth shut.

Make a hole on each side of the circle and thread a piece of string through. Twist the string as tightly as you can, then let it unwind as you hold the string taut between your fingers. The circle will spin around. What happens to the dog?

Answers
1. **False** (Champollion was the first to figure out how to read hieroglyphics, the writing of the Ancient Egyptians.)
2. **False** (The first text he printed was the Bible.)
3. **True** (Thomas Edison became deaf at age 14.)
4. **True**
5. **False** (Anthracite is the highest quality. It is harder and has been underground longer.)
6. **True**
7. **False** (Lasers have uses in printing, medicine, compact disc players, and more!)

■ Did you know?

Gunpowder

Just like paper and the compass, gunpowder was an invention of the Chinese. They used it to make flaming arrows in wartime and fireworks. The Mongols stole the secret formula from the Chinese and passed it to the Arabs, who used it against the Europeans during the Crusades. The world's very first cannons were used in Europe in the 15th century.

Fireworks

The Scandinavians taught us to ski! People

in cold mountain regions had always used skis to get around on snow. In 1888 the Norwegian Nansen crossed Greenland on skis. The sport was developed as techniques of turning and racing were perfected. The first international skiing competition was held in 1921.

Anesthetic, used to put patients to sleep for operations, was first used in 1846 in Boston, Massachusetts, by Dr. William Morton. Earlier, in 1841, Charles Jackson had discovered that ether could be used as an anesthetic.

The X ray was discovered in 1895 by the German physicist Wilhelm Roentgen. Soon doctors began using X rays to see inside the human body. In 1903, the German surgeon George Perthes discovered that X rays slow down or stop the growth of cancer. Today doctors use X-ray treatments to fight many forms of cancer; we call it radiotherapy.

Louis Pasteur, the French chemist who gave his name to pasteurization, began developing vaccines in 1879. He discovered that if weakened bacteria were injected into the body, the bacteria stimulated the body's own defenses to protect it from illness. Thanks to vaccines, doctors can immunize people against many of the most dangerous diseases known, including smallpox, tuberculosis, tetanus, diphtheria, polio, and rabies.

Penicillin was named by Alexander Fleming in 1928. He noticed that a mold had killed some of the bacteria on a dish in his laboratory. He found that the mold produced a substance that killed certain bacteria in humans without damaging white blood cells. It was an important milestone in the history of treatment of disease and infection: antibiotics had been discovered.

The refrigerator was a brilliant idea! If food is chilled it can be stored and kept fresh much longer than if it is left at room temperature. Long ago, people realized that ice is useful. In medieval times, people collected ice in winter and buried it in deep holes. Later, ships were sent to bring pieces of icebergs to European ports.

About 1850, scientists found that low temperatures could be created through chemical procedures. Charles Tellier, a Frenchman, invented a refrigerator that used ammonia; as it dissolved in water, the ammonia absorbed heat and produced cold.

Who invented matches? Until the middle of the 19th century, people lit candles with slender tapers soaked in sulfur, which had to be touched to another flame. In 1830 in France, Charles Suria added white phosphorus to the tip of a small stick of wood, which ignited when struck against a surface coated with sulfur and potassium chlorate. But because white phosphorus is poisonous, it was later replaced by red phosphorus. Modern matches had been invented.

■ Inventors of genius

Many inventors of crucial inventions, landmarks of progress, remain anonymous or are lost in legend. But the names of more recent inventors are well known.

Johannes Gutenberg (1398–1467)

He was German and a goldsmith by trade. The Chinese had invented printing, but Gutenberg discovered the most practical way to use it. In Europe, people were already printing with wood engravings. Gutenberg invented movable metal type, which he fixed on a frame. Letters could be rearranged and reused.

Jacques Daguerre (1787–1851)

In 1835, together with Nicephore Niepce, he worked on methods for developing photographs. The films he used were copper plates coated with silver iodide; these turned black when exposed to light and recorded an image. To develop the image, Daguerre first dipped the plate in another chemical, then fixed it with a solution of common salt.

Samuel Morse (1791–1872)

An American painter, he later became an inventor. He perfected a system of transmitting messages by means of electric signals. His alphabet, known as Morse Code, was made up simply of short dots and long dashes. It could be read, heard, or seen from a distance; it has been useful in the shipping business. The letters SOS (three short, three long, three short) form the international distress signal.

Thomas Edison (1847–1931)

Born into a poor family, he started his career by selling newspapers, but by the time he died, he had many inventions to his name. At the age of 14, he became deaf, but this disability did not stop him from inventing the phonograph in 1877. It was a device that could reproduce sounds. A cylinder turned, and a needle reproduced the vibrations made by a human voice. Edison also founded the first cinema studio.

Alexander Graham Bell (1847–1922)

Born in Scotland, he started by teaching sign language to children who could not hear or speak. As he tried different ways of helping people who were hearing impaired, he concentrated on the vibrations the human voice makes. He succeeded in transmitting a sound down an electric wire, and this led to the invention of the telephone in 1876.

Rudolph Diesel (1858–1913)

He began his career as a refrigeration engineer. He noticed that the steam engines of his day were not very powerful, and, in 1893, he attempted the first experiments with an engine that worked on fuel oil, igniting by compression of air and not from an electric spark. He has given his name to all engines that work on diesel fuel.

Gertrude Elion (1918–)

In 1944 she went to work for a pharmaceutical company in New York. Although she started as a lab assistant, she soon began working with the other scientists. Throughout her career, she developed a series of drugs that have become essential in treating heart disease, ulcers, and leukemia. In 1988, she was awarded the Nobel Peace Prize in physiology and medicine.

Women have invented many of the objects we see or use every day, including: Harriet Tracy, who invented the fire escape in 1883; Josephine Cochran, who invented the dishwashing machine in 1886; Mary Anderson, who invented the windshield wiper in 1903; Eva Landman, who invented the modern umbrella in 1935; and Bette Nesmith Graham, who invented Liquid Paper in 1950.

Diesel engines are more efficient than gasoline engines, but tend to be quite heavy. They are mainly used in large vehicles.

■ Glossary

Amber: fossilized resin. Its Greek name, electron, gives us the word "electricity."

Aluminum: a soft, light-weight metal, often used in aircraft bodies.

Cam: a piece of wood or metal fit into a wheel that transforms circular motion into up-and-down motion or vice versa.

Caravel: small, sturdy boat with three sails, riding high in the water and carrying a crew of about 20.

Circuit (electric): wire pathway, usually copper, that carries electricity to and from a power source.

Cosmos: the universe seen as an ordered whole, from the Greek word "kosmos," meaning "world."

Crank: rod bent at right angles for converting a circular movement to an up-and-down motion.

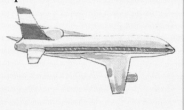

Domesticate: to tame. Pigs, cows, sheep, and goats were once wild animals that people domesticated over the centuries. People first domesticated horses 4,000 years ago.

Economy: the organized system by which a society orders its banking, industry, and commerce.

Environmentalist: someone whose study and work involve caring for Earth and safeguarding the future of all living things.

Forge: to shape metal by heating it in fire and hammering it as it cools.

Fossil: plant or animal remains that have been preserved in the ground for many thousands of years until they turned to stone, but which can be recognized for what they were.

Gauge: the distance between the rails of a railroad line. The standard gauge for most European countries is about five feet (1.4 m). Before the gauge was standardized, early railway engineers encountered many problems. What were they to do when rails of two different companies met? Passengers and freight had to be loaded and then reloaded, a tiresome business.

Hawker: a traveling salesperson. Centuries ago, when stores were still rare, hawkers went from town to town selling needles and thread, lace, pots, and books.

Interest: the sum of money a borrower pays to the lender in addition to the amount of a loan.

Latitude: position on the Earth north or south of the Equator.

Longitude: position on the Earth east or west of the Greenwich Meridian.

Mine: to dig into the ground to extract metal or

coal. Open-cast mines exploit metal or coal reserves near the surface. Deeper reserves need to be mined via a vertical shaft cut into the ground.

Nugget: small rough lump of natural gold or other precious metal.

Orbit: repeated, curved course of a planet or satellite around another object in space. To orbit something means to go around it. Our planet Earth orbits the sun.

Phoenicians: people of a great trading nation covering part of what is now Lebanon and Syria in the Middle East, at the height of their power from the 14th to the ninth centuries B.C. Through trade, they linked the old civilizations of Egypt and Mesopotamia with the newer powers in the Mediterranean. They even traveled as far as Cornwall, in England.

Photoelectric cells: a device that uses light energy to produce an electrical effect. These cells are used in electronic eyes for automatic doors and in exposure meters for photography.

Photovoltaic cells: devices that produce direct electric current by chemical action (as in a battery). They are recharged by light. They were first made for spacecraft, but now they often power watches or pocket calculators.

Porcelain: fine, delicate china made from white clay called kaolin mixed with powdered granite.

Spices: extracts of aromatic plants used to flavor food. Some examples are ginger, cumin, cinnamon, and cloves. Many grow in countries with hot climates.

Starboard: the right-hand side of a ship. Before the invention of the stern rudder, ships were steered by a

rudder on the right, or "steerboard" side. This became "starboard." Because of the projecting rudder, it was impossible for a ship to tie up at port on that side, so the other side, the left, became known as the port side.

Stock exchange: a large place where stocks and shares in businesses around the world are bought and sold. The London Stock Exchange is the oldest in the world.

Subsoil: soil lying just below the surface soil, often of poor quality.

Tidal power station: when an estuary channels the motion of the tides, the tides produce a strong flow of water. Tidal power is harnessed by building a dam across the tidal flow. Some environmentalists object to this form of power, saying it damages the wetlands and the wildfowl that depend on them for habitat.

Typeset: to arrange letters and spaces ready for printing on a press. Skilled compositors used to put movable type in place, one letter at a time. Today, printers rely on computers for much of the typesetting.

Valve: a sort of plug that opens and closes automatically.

Watt: electrical unit of power named after the inventive Scottish engineer, James Watt.

Wavelength: distance from the crest of one wave to the crest of the next wave.

Here is a list of other books to read to find out more about inventions. Visit your library or a local bookstore to find more titles.

Experimenting with Inventions by R. Gardner (Franklin Watts, 1990).

Futuristics: A Time to Come by J. Tanner (Zephyr Press, 1992).

Great Lives: Invention and Technology by M. Lomask (Macmillan Children's Book Group, 1991).

Ideas That Changed the World: The Greatest Discoveries and Inventions by R. Igpen and P. Wilkinson (Chelsea House, 1994).

Inventing for Kids by E.A. Brubaker and D.R. Garmire (Synergetics, 1992).

Inventing Things by J. Brown and M. Holt (Gareth Stevens, 1990).

Inventions by D. Sylvester (Learning Works, 1992).

Inventions: Inventors and Ingenious Ideas by P. Turvey (Franklin Watts, 1992).

Inventive Genius (Silver Burdett, 1993).

Mistakes That Worked by C.F. Jones (Doubleday, 1991).

The Picture History of Great Inventors by G. Clements (Knopf Books for Young Readers, 1994).

Samuel Todd's Book of Great Inventions by E.L. Konigsburg (Macmillan Children's Book Group, 1991).

Wacky Inventions: How Things Work in the Modern World by Andrews and McMeel (Turner, 1993).

The Way Things Work by D. Macaulay (Houghton Mifflin, 1988).

The Weird and Wondrous World of Patents by R.O. Richardson (Sterling, 1990).

What Does It Do?: Inventions Then and Now by D. Jacobs (Raintree Steck-Vaughn Publishers, 1990).

The Wright Brothers by R.M. Haynes (Silver Burdett, 1990).

Also check out Creative Education's *It's A Fact!* titles, *Earth and Space* and *Great Inventions*, and our *Images* series, which includes these titles: *Air Pollution, Bacteria, Cells, Galaxies, Mars, Moon, Stars, Space Exploration,* and *The Sun.*

Perhaps after reading this book about other people's inventions, you would like to become an inventor. You start with an idea—how can you make something better? How can you complete an activity or chore faster? Draw a picture of your invention and give it a name.

Some schools or community centers have associations or clubs for people interested in becoming inventors. Look for listings in your phone book or ask around at your school. Here is a place to write to for information on becoming an inventor:

Invent America!
U.S. Patent Model Foundation
1505 Powhatan Street
Alexandria, VA 22314

This organization sponsors the Invent America! competitions in elementary and middle schools. Write for their packet of information for your school.

INDEX

The entries in **bold** refer to whole chapters on the subject.